To my grandson,

JACK xxx

HAPPY BIRTHDAY

From

NA NA e PAW PAW xxxxxx

HAPPY BIRTHDAY

......................................, which piñata has the sweets inside?

Shake the book really fast....

Come on, ...,
let's **POP** the balloons.

Ready?
Steady?
Go!

Press here
....

READY? STEADY? SMILE....

Time for a funny birthday selfie,

....

IT'S MY BIRTHDAY

HA, HA, ..., it's upside down!

Turn the book to see who's monkeying around.

Ready for your
big present,
...........................?

Tilt the book this way....

To my
grandson,

Happy Birthday,

.........................!

Now take a big
breath in and
BLOW
out your candles.

3,
2, 1...

MY FAVOURITE PARTY GAME IS:

HAPPY BIRTHDAY

MY AMAZING PARTY GUESTS ARE CALLED:

Draw your cake

Illustrated by
Hazel Quintanilla
Designed by
Steph Clark

First published by
Orangutan Books in 2020
1 Queen Street,
Bath BA1 1HE

@orangutanbooks

Copyright © Orangutan Books Ltd 2020
ISBN 978-1-83883-460-9
All rights reserved
Printed in China
OB_PO202005